Robert
Ferguson

Start
to
Finish

novum pro

This book is also
available as
e-book.

www.novum-publishing.co.uk

© 2022 novum publishing

ISBN 978-3-99131-754-8
Editing: Atarah Yarach, DipEdit
Cover photos: Sergey Kolesnikov,
Meinzahn, Elen33,
Denys Bilytskyi | Dreamstime.com
Cover design, layout & typesetting:
novum publishing

www.novum-publishing.co.uk

Climate neutral
Print product
ClimatePartner.com/16547-2201-1002

Contents

Acknowledgements

The following poems were first published in various editions of "The Cannon's Mouth", the quarterly anthology of Cannon Poets. They are reproduced here by kind permission.

"Second Sunrise", *"Tomorrow"*, *"What Have I Done?"*, *"Orpheus and Eurydice"*, and *"Winter Walking"*

Introduction

It is four years since the publication of my first collection, "Late Starter", and I seem to have collected many more poems, so perhaps it is time for another.

As befits my advancing years, this one is something of a biography, with chronological and meteorological additions. It begins with memories of my boyhood and culminates in contemplations of a very happy and surprisingly active old age. Threaded through the content, the theme of time is recorded by reference to months and seasons, between which a number of notable national events are recorded. The COVID pandemic (2020-2022, and ongoing, though hopefully not for much longer) seemed at first to be a time of isolation, but in fact became a time of national and international online meetings with people from places we would not have dreamed of visiting, stimulating almost more inspirations for poetry than in the preceding busy, mobile years.

At the same time, groups of poets met online, and this collection owes much to the example and guidance of members of Cannon Poets of Birmingham, the neighbouring Solihull Writers Workshop, and Leicestershire's Brightsparks Arts, to say nothing of the enthusiastic support of Midlands Poets Laureate, in particular Charlie Jordan. Hence, from time to time, poems appear here in various arcane structures from haiku and tanka to sestina and rondeau redouble, and almost everything between. Rhyming patterns, lay-outs, and stanza- and line-lengths vary, as a result of my having been encouraged to play with words and "see what came out." The reader must judge their success. For me, they provide more pleasure than crossword puzzles or Wordle, but each to their own.

No one enjoys every poem in a collection equally, but hopefully everyone may find something in this one which they can enjoy, perhaps remember (if only in part), or something which makes them recall a similar experience of their own, and perhaps begin to write themselves for their own pleasure, and that of others.

Robert Ferguson,
Spring 2022.

Earthquake in Peterborough

We had an earthquake last night. In Peterborough.
Never heard of Peterborough? Not surprised.
Not much ever happens here, you may be sure.
Some people go through it, quickly, in trains
From London to Scotland or the other way on.
It stands here with the flat Fens on one side
And the low Midland hills on the other.
Not the place for an earthquake, you'd say.
Not that my Mum or Dad, or I, noticed it happening,
Only, Miss Tweddle our teacher said it had,
And some of the class, so I suppose it must have done.
Shook cups off their dresser, Billy Knowles said,
But then it would have to have happened to him, wouldn't it?
I'm sorry to have missed it, I must say,
But perhaps there'll be another one sometime soon.

The Library Burned to the Ground

Nobody knows who did it, if anyone did, or nobody's saying.
It wasn't much, poor thing.
Just a square brick building with a flat roof,
One room inside, lots of windows, and a "cloakroom"
The librarian called it, giving you the key
When you were enjoying yourself too much and got caught short.
No-one was hurt in the fire.
The librarian lady had gone home on her bike at seven o'clock,
As usual. But so much was lost.
Only a little branch library in a suburb
A bus ride from the big library in the town.
Perhaps they'll rebuild it, restock it,
But the person who purchased most of the books is long gone
And their choices, their classics, their memories
Won't be repeated,
And I loved them, stars, classics and new.
Just, that collection has moulded me,
Made me what I am, built up my values
Since my Dad took me in, far too tiny,
Ignoring the desk-lady's scowl at the notice
About "no children under 8 years of age"

How They Brought the Good News

The first ascent of Mt. Everest, by Sir Edmund Hillary and Tensing Norgay in June 1953, was the subject of exuberant celebration across the world. In the United Kingdom, school children were taken to their local cinema – at public expense! – to see the film of the assault which had been taken from the Base Camp several miles below the summit.

The screen extends infinitely to left and right
Spear-sharp silver slices the hard blue sky
Camera closes in on mountains' armour
Gullies pattern vertical shades of grey
Two tiny dots of black appear creeping
Like flies slowly upwards
Joined by a cotton thread
One bends to carve a step beside his knee
And then another and another, rests
Stretches carefully, flails his axe again
Companion lifts a tired foot, rises
Up the wall, pauses again and tightens
The umbilical that joins them
And then a widening band of blue
Appears above them, and the first fly
Hauls himself, bent, over the snowy edge
Turns and takes in the thread and his companion
Onto the very ceiling of the world.
Flags fly, teeth flash from beards and hoods
Amidst the pride and the worldwide applause

Waterfall, Betws-y-Coed

We walked down the valley by the quiet brown stream,
Becoming aware of a growing growl,
Then deafening, frightening, ROARING,
And we only see why when we walk past
The white rock threshold that crosses the valley
Down which the stream throws itself, bodily,
Now grown up, much wider, its white curls streaming
Down its face and into its frothing basin
                  And on down the valley, wider but calmer
                  We follow it, adult now, off to the sea.

The Dance Class

He's a gent! He doesn't hold me close
Even in the darkest corners. Even when we turn.
If only he knew, if only he could sense,
How very much I need to feel his body
To give me notice where to put my feet,
Feel his arms, his chest, his thighs. He's very sweet.
I'm sure he needs to feel me too.
Too conscious of his need, too fearful of my judgement
But oh, if only he were conscious that, for me,
Our needs are one.

Weather for Ducks

Will we go to the flicks, he asked her
Easily, sure of himself
And what will we see, she countered sharp
That new one, they say it's great
How shall I come, she asked, if it rains
Expect you at six, he said
Remember the idea was all yours
For I shan't in bad weather
Or if the cat dies, she insisted
Remember your hood, he said
Don't think I don't know why you asked me
Unlock those chains, he said

Come Friday, outside the cinema
Keeping an eye on the sky
She stood in the rain disappointed

Flawed Diamond

Kimberley by name as well as nature
Gifted, sparkling with internal light
Drawn from rough earth, stood proud among her peers.
Once cut, she shattered, now worth but a shrug.
Why do we not examine our desires,
Especially their origins, before
We dream of fortunes not within our grasp?

The Teacher

I will build my empire, not with violence
Or with the imposition of my values, my laws and my rules,
But gently, by persuasion,
Gathering examples and advantages
And presenting them for the benefit of those who'll listen.

Not everyone will, just then.
Young George, whose empire is on YouTube,
Whose army is his drummer, his bass and rhythm players,
His sisters who sing "Whoo-oo" at the end of every verse.
But maybe somewhere, someday,
I will give him something useful
That he may not recognise for years
And then one day he'll remember
And that's how, just occasionally,
My empire grows.

February

Listen to February crawling by
Dripping down the front wall from the broken gutter
No footsteps, no-one passing
The robin's there outside but does not sing
No other bird invades his territory
The gate is frozen closed, its hinges silent.
All is asleep, and soon so shall I be.

Mystery

Lake mirrors hills and clouds
Willows bend to shield water
What does your hair hide?

Chilled

February rain
Cold as ice down your collar
Straightening your back

Orpheus and Eurydice

Don't do it, friend. You are no Orpheus
However sweet your voice, how skilled your playing.
It is a myth, and, like all such, a lesson
Which says there is no future in the past.
Your time may come to re-invent, revisit
What you have lost, the errors you have made,
Once you are laid below, not to return.
They cannot be repaired, only rehurt,
In this life. All you can do is learn
And not repeat. What's done is done.
Your Eurydice has moved on, and you.
By now you are both different. Don't look back.

My Beautiful Boy

Bricks loosen in ancient walls. Roofs fall.
Bridges collapse. Cars burst into flames.
Unsinkable ships founder with massive loss of life.
Birds die out, and poachers kill off rhinos for their tusks.
All these are tragedies, and so is mine.

My beautiful boy has a problem.
A chromosome has not developed
And he will never grow up as others do.
Computers blip. "Switch off, then on",
And everything continues as before.
I can't do that for my beautiful boy.
He will never be "normal", and not that for very long.
It is not my fault, they tell me. It happens.
We don't know why it has happened for him
And not for the boy of the mum in my neighbouring bed.
Creation is not perfect. Then what's the point?
So we make up myths to try to explain
The as-yet inexplicable, find a blame.
In a decade, century, two, we might have reasons
And be able to stop it.
But my beautiful boy will never be as others,
Will never talk, smile, respond as others do.

He will have a hard life.
At least he won't know it,
But I will, and I grieve for him, still with us,
And love, care, and protect him
For as long as we have him. He is our gift.
My beautiful, beautiful boy.

Changeable, Ain't It?

cloud like pastry rolls across the grey sky
west wind will blow it eastward by and by
rivers return within their banks   hedges appear
the field once lake becomes a shallow mere

sun rises slowly   mud dries brown and hard
falls from abandoned cows far from their yard
soaked sheep bleat plaintively for lambs long lost
icicles hang from fleeces in the frost
and yet in hours the yellow spring warmth comes
to change the world   grass sprouts   the cold succumbs
fledglings creep out from mothers' warming breasts
squeak   whistle   test their gifts beyond the nests

two days of sunshine   what can they expect
more before cloud and drizzle disconnect
ocean and continent on either hand
it grows from where we are   this is our land

Spring

Snowline climbs uphill
Retreating as warmth expands
Will you soon return?

Ukraine, 5th March, 2022

Sunflowers stand proudly in the corn
Heads waving to the blast of bombs
Hitting the defenceless village.

What is seen from skyward aircraft,
Impregnable? Clustered houses,
Still, deserted tractors scattered
In the fields, bodies here and there.

A shattered wall formerly hid
Grandparents now too old to run
Parched, starved, hopeless, can only wait
For soldiers jumping from their truck
Afraid, armed, tasked to clear the road
And all that moves, that threatens.
They will spray death here in the corn
Among the sunflower heads that wave
To no one. No one's there to see.

Orographia

The cloud
crossing sea
was content to
grow, collecting wet
drops the waves threw upwards
until it reached hills
which forced it high
dropping rain
in floods

Beyond
it sank down
warmed, dried, dispersed
permitting the sun
to roast the land
always dry
below

The Dresser Drawer

At the corner of the dresser in the kitchen is a drawer.
It sticks, and then comes out when you pull too hard.
But it doesn't really matter, 'cos there's nothing useful in it.
It's where we put the things we haven't time to put away
Or can't remember where we put the other one of them
When we last had one, ages and ages ago.
One day I opened it, well, pulled it hard
And bent to pick its contents off the floor.
One end of a plastic mousetrap, 'cos Mum can't bear
Either mice or killing, but split the other end.
A forty-page instruction book for a Japanese radio
Which died when VHF came in, and brother Fred
Cannibalised it for spare parts – the radio, not the leaflet,
Though whether the instructions were in English
Korean, Japanese or ancient Greek no one decided.
There was a screwdriver sticking up from the floor,
Nearly from my toe, the point so sharp
It couldn't possibly have turned a screw-head.
Two copper-knob batteries rolled across the vinyl. Another disappeared
Beneath the gas stove. So did one of the pastilles
Which came loose from a half-used strip
Stuck to the sticky side of a tube of sun-cream
Beside a tiny picture-hook, bright, brassy, with no nail.
A pair of pliers. Dad leaped on them, exultant.
"Who put them there?" he demanded. "You," said Mum.
"I watched you do it last weekend," she told him,
Picking up the half-opened Elastoplast,
And throwing it in the bin.

More or Less?

All it needs is cutting
Or not cutting
Itches a bit if it isn't washed
After a day or two
But doesn't object too much
If it's left a week
Can be left to its own creativity
Shaved or part-shaved or not shaved at all
Or totally harvested, cleared like a clean-ploughed field
Stark, bare, denuded, without fence or hedge
Just the top of my body
The lighthouse of what is me.

.

Weather

February fill dyke   April showers
Autumn's Indian Summer   Carol singers' snow
Red sky morning and night
listen to the Old Men's judgements
generalised but eventually accurate
drawn from generations of observations of
castellated clouds   sodden fields   a bee's buzz
absences of birds and silence of their songs
from doors and windows of houses built
above the floods   south-facing for the sun
small windowed   sheltered from the cold north winds
driven by jet-streams we didn't know existed fifty years before
and cannot control despite
being able to walk on the moon

Summer

Back then
In long hot days
I wandered far from home
To shaven fields where muscled men
Heaved sheaves

And forked
The corn up high
To colleagues sweating hard
On threshers driven by steaming
Machines

Combines
Like red houses
Dominate the fields now
Chasing the scared hares and field mice
To death

Lorries
Line up to take
Grain from one side. Black wraps
Of plastic sausage are spilled out
Like waste

But gone
Is human sign
Except for me leaning
On the far gate in the sweltering
Hot sun

Only coolth
By the river
Shallow gravelled water.
Float drifts. Hook ignored by fish and folk
I Doze.

Yorkshire Morning

Sky navy blue, star-spangled,
Hornsea beach of flints from Flamborough Head.
Bench to sit, table for flask and cup
For comfort and warmth after an early run.
Low tide, flat sea, grey to a far horizon
Clarifying as the blue fades,
Wakening sleeping seagulls, drifting calmly.
Brief orange streaks herald a tangerine rising
Like a stage backdrop, growing, brightening,
Blinding, to begin another day.

Jury Rigged

Around the bulwark a magenta line
Scratched by the nets jerked overboard
In the casting, lodged between winch and catch
                until unjammed
Scratches defining the journal of each trip

Senses

Without sight I am unsure
Without hearing I am in danger
Without taste or smell I am unstimulated
Without touch I am lonely

The Pomegranate Hotel
(Hotel Garanat, Granada, Andalucia)

None of the walls in my hotel room are straight
None join the wooden ceiling at a right-angle
And the ceiling slopes. Lintels are twenty centimetres
Square, of solid oak, but hardly horizontal
And the carved, fretted shutters filter out the heat
With shadows playful on my high-raised bed
As the hot sun moves round.

Outside my door, from the tiled courtyard cooled
By its fountain-bath, floors rise in tiers
Each one surrounded by a balcony of timber.
Down below, the cellar dining-room is barrel-ceilinged.
Slotted windows light our communal table
From too high for us to see the feet
Which tap or shuffle by incessantly.

This was a pilgrim refuge years ago.
Pilgrims still come for hospitality,
For guidance and for sleep after a long day
Seeking the enigmatic experiences
Of those who traipse the city's crowded ways.

The Passage of Time

Nearly a century since the war in which I was born
My father would not recognise this age
If he were recreated new today
Then we were stratified, then each knew his place
Duty and service, climb up if you could
Avoiding debt and shame, to be respected
For ability and success
If not for what your family never were

Then there was a wide world, fought for, conquered
Europe a place of varied difference
Food, drink, language, mystery and myth
The origin of our culture and our values
Beyond to north, cold lands of ice and snow
To south of desert, river, forest, heat
To be explored, abandoned piece by piece
As we grew up, tested ourselves against the world

Now everywhere's accessible for pleasure
Trunks and bikinis on the Red Sea coast
In leisure's name we travel, or in profit's,
Because we can, texting, face-timing relatives and friends

Cornish Idyll

As you approach, the road gets narrow.
Hedges close in, on turfed then rocky walls.
The street is entered. Tiny shops with doors
Too low for foreign men. Narrow and dark
Converted cottages. Gay umbrellas
And café tables front them, rails hold them
Back against the sheer slope up which they clawed
Three centuries ago. Curved cliffs almost surround
A minute bay, closed by pier heads and foam,
In which toy boats roll gently to their buoys,
And, over all, the smells of salt and fish
And vinegar and sweat and petrol fumes
All swelter in the sun. Different from home,
A sharper, brighter, more relaxing sun.

The Skipper's Nightmare

The captain strode the stern deck, whence all but he had fled.
The rain poured down. He pulled his cap more firmly on his head.
Before him, a full seventy feet of steel stretched out ahead.

He twitched the tiller left then right, to counteract the wind.
The channel bent again, he thought. The rain near' made him blind.
He had to steer by guess and God. Another boat behind.

His panic rose. He cut the revs, moved over to the right.
Bushes and trees o'erhung the stream. The bend was very tight.
He'd let the other pass and lead them on, without a fight.

The boat behind came on a-pace. It's horn blared in his ears.
The angle to the approaching bridge was sharp. The captain's fears
Increased. He throttled back again, and heard the other's jeers.

As his competitor swung past, he realised what they'd do.
The other boat swung hard across. The captain called his crew,
"Hold on. We can't stop. We'll collide!" Disaster loomed, he knew.

There was a crash. The captain felt deep pain right up his arm.
He thought, "I wonder whether someone else has come to harm?"
But, as he woke, he gradually regained his usual calm.

"T'was but a dream," he realised, relaxing on the floor
Where rolling from his narrow bed had laid him, he was sure.
"It didn't happen. Oh, praise be! In fact, I'm safe ashore."

Taking off and hanging up the cap he'd worn in bed,
He promised that, in future, never mind what others said,
He'd give up hopes of boating, find another dream instead.

Morning Walk

My cat and I go for a walk each morning.
She wears her braces proudly
And ignores her lead (no dog)
To trot across the garden
By my foot, sniffing a daffodil
A raspberry
A cabbage leaf
Briefly
To the back gate and into the horses' field
Where she stops
To sit and regard the world
Through amber eyes
Ears pricked to check for threats
For opportunities
For something to explore.
In summer, butterflies demand attack.
In winter, frost coats grass stems
With cold dampness, causing her
To lift each paw in turn
Delicately
Before returning it separately to earth
And lifting the other
Turning her head, ensuring I am there
In case she needs to leap for cover
On my chest
Claws giving purchase
In the strong fabric of my anorak
And so be carried home.

Atlases

In my library is my father's atlas
And one of mine.
His is out of date. Cities, whole countries,
Have changed their names from those that empires gave them,
Drew their borders straight.
Now they are bent, or totally expunged,
Where people, tribes, whole nations
Have crossed them and extended
Their politics and their influence,
Their roads and railways,
Industries, farms and towns.
My atlas shows these changes
But my grandson has an atlas which is different from mine.

The Box

The box arrived on Tuesday in the front hall
No-one remembered ordering it at all
The silence that greeted it was a dying fall

We all ignored the box for several days
As if we suffered from an insane craze
We told the gardener to put it in the maze

But he feared dissolution in inclement rainy weather
So we brought it inside, and waited to see
Whether it would open itself. We encouraged its endeavour.

By Friday, it had begun to smell. Not the box,
But what was in it. Visits by the local feral fox
Suggested meat of some sort rather than assorted grubby socks

We opened it on Sunday. That seemed best.
The stink was rabid. John stripped to his vest
To do the job. He looked in, let it rest.

He closed the box. We asked him, "What's in there?"
John just turned green, and said, "Don't want to share."
Wrapped in thick plastic, we left it at the local Fayre.

Squabbles on the Towpath

PAINTER

Knotted, wet, uncoiled
Thrown to land at partner's feet
Another row done

BARGE POLE

Dip, push, gurgle, heave, sweat
Mud swirls in disturbed water
No progress, still stuck

MOORHEN

Red beak between reeds
Paddling feet accelerate
Fear on calm waters

HAWTHORN

White blossoms hide birds
Hear them call where they are safe
She hides and squeaks too

Second Sunrise

"Look what I found, Mama!" he was calling,
Excited, as he skipped towards me,
The Thing dancing in his arms with every step.
"Look what I found in the field," he was calling
When he tripped, and it fell, and the sun rose
For the second time that morning,
And my sight went black in the flash,
And when I got up and could see, dimly,
He had disappeared from the earth,
From my life,
For ever.

Who left that there for my beautiful child to find?
Who sold that thing which destroyed my son, my hope?
Who gave their life to making that terrible thing?
Should they not be terribly ashamed?

Late September

Hot high sun declining, evenings drawing in,
Tickle of chill in the morning as the duvet is pushed back,
Drawn up again and reluctantly pushed aside.
Reach for the bedside light, first time since……
Warmth in the radiator, only slight but there.
Dig out the lightweight jumper from the topmost drawer.
Summer's passing.

The Medium

"I have a message for someone in that corner."
Everyone scraped their chair an inch from her focus,
But we were too crowded in upon each other.
There was no escape.
"The blonde lady with the green scarf.
Do not worry for your mother. The spirit is a man,
An older man, who has already passed. He says
He is waiting to welcome her,
And you will have to grieve
Again, as you did for him, but it will pass
As it did before.
He says, You have a life.
Go out and live it, duty done
By both of us."
She was in tears, but comforted.
And I, who knew her and her Mum
In hospital,
Was shaken to my core.

The Blue Peacock

The blue peacock stands on one leg to claw
At the blue blossoms on the bush before
Its beak, just at the vase's porcelain curve,
Turns smoothly round to flash reflecting light.

Once, as his fingers raised the clay, he watched
The bird, perhaps, and knew what had inspired
His hands and eyes that morning, dreaming as
The blue peacock stands on one leg to claw.

Across the garden, where he works his wheel,
Eyes half-closed, fingers loose so he can feel
The cool clay turning, seeing in his mind
Its beak, just at the vase's porcelain curve.

Once fired and cooled and handled, glazes mixed,
He settles down to reproduce the fixed
Image he has held, picks up the vase,
Turns smoothly round to flash reflecting light.

Standing among the clutter left to pack,
The vase stands on its shelf, pushed to the back,
Soon to begin another journey to
A new home, to be seen and be unseen.

Voyager 2

Locked down, how far away seem the surroundings
Once so familiar; streets, shops, neighbours
Just a step, a mile or two, away,
The family an outpost thirty, forty miles
Along well-travelled roads, now inaccessible,
And we are lonely in our separate rooms.
Think for a moment. Twelve billion miles beyond
What we can see, past all the stars we've plotted
In a summer sky, suns, planets, black holes,
Constellations, a tiny pod plods on and out,
Its sides lit only briefly by reflection
As it passes yet another nuclear fire,
Leaves it behind. Occasionally, "ping"
It says, and "ping" comes back from Earth
If it waits long enough, as though
The bread were passed a full half-hour
After it was requested.
We think we're lonely? Does it think out there?
Do feelings die, or maybe generate
After so long alone in blackness?
How lonely is that tiny metal babe?

Our Autumn

Sad Autumn. Leaves' lives over
Shorter than most of ours
Collapsing from consciousness on their twigs
Photosynthesising as they were formed to do.
That formation gone, as ours will be
Drifting into unseeing, unknowing nothingness
Dropping and being dropped, bare or encoffined,
Onto and into the ground,
Things to let go, as trees let go of leaves?

Feet

Faraway feet, enclosed, unsafe,
Though armoured, trying to flatten the ground
And all opposition. Used to be under control
For running and kicking, not knowing then
The nerves, like marionettes' strings,
Like aeroplanes' wires from joystick to ailerons, rudders and flaps,
Controlled the whole body, including my feet.
Not now.

Beyond Real

I sat at last
Able to tuck up my feet into my knees after so many years
Following complex paths set by others centuries before
For the comfort and the security
Of their needs
And looked within
Beyond reality
To the Light.
Why had it taken me so long?
Now release was instant, in a flash,
The knowledge that the values placed on anything
By human judgement
Were of no importance,
Except what I could see with my closed eyes.

What have I done?

Numb, since the Officer raised me to my feet
Shaking, having heard the dreadful word
"Guilty". Now the Judge's sentence
"Eighteen years", a life-time
Numb, as I'm turned around and pushed
Down the steep narrow stair
Into the white van's tiny cabin
Sit on the metal seat, locked in
Numb, without thought, my brain a mush
At Reception, "Strip". Pain at the search
"Dress". Cold denim. Pushed
From hand to hand. "You know the way"
Corridor, steel stair, another,
Cell door. "Sit". Door closed and locked
Incarcerated. Eighteen years
I will be here
Can I stay numb a lifetime?
Will I go mad?

Social Media

What if everyone started acting,
Expressing themselves in mime?
They might, if everything we said
Were recorded for all time.

So, after forty years or more,
Someone, to criticise,
Could call your curse from the archive.
Wouldn't that be a surprise?

"Oh, surely not! I couldn't have said
Such awful words as that!"
"You did," they say, and prove it.
Your conscience would knock you flat.

Who could possibly preach a sermon?
Who could possibly make a speech?
But isn't that where we've got to?
Isn't this what the media teach?

Storm

Layer by layer
The cloud climbs up ever up
Throws lightning to earth
Your anger flashes
Splitting our friendship

The Sinking Ship

Sawn at and frayed, the paper painter gave,
The battered dinghy floated from the quay.
Where were the parents? Reaching out to save?
No, careless all, as if they could not see.

Stout oarsmen in the midships pulled and bawled
War-cries and mottos, "Onwards. Get it done."
Kilted, the bowmen wept. "Return!" they called,
"We are shanghaied," but still the boat ploughed on.

Six counties in the stern were torn and sank
As from the quay the frail craft ripped away.
Alternate documents like party pranks
Rose on the waves and drifted o'er the bay.

"Where are we going?" "Away from there! It's great!
To freedom, to a land of money-trees,
Where no-one will say no, no-one dictate,
We'll sell and buy and gather in fat fees!"

"But what if no-one wants to trade with us,
Or we can't make the things we used to do?"
"Poo, poo, my boy, be plucky. Why this fuss?
They'll love us as they always used to do."

And so the battered dinghy drifted on,
Leaking and sinking deeper in the waves
Until, unguided, an automaton,
It disappeared with us, unwilling slaves.

Loving Venice

To come to love Venice, forget
Your fear of sore feet and getting lost.
They will beset you, but ignore them.

Seek out the *calli*, shaded by the walls
Of palaces painted ochre by the years of sun.
Seek out the bridges, up and down again.

Here a *piazza* opens, with a central well
And cafés on the side beyond the sun,
A cat stretched nonchalantly on a windowsill.

La Serenissima, always a surprise
Around each corner, along each canal quay,
And, when you tire, a boat to get you home.

Winter Walking

From the front door I scuttle, duffle coat fastened

On both remaining horns, hood round my wool-encrusted ears

Inside my pulled-down hat to keep ice crystals out of greying hair,

Three pairs of socks and newish rubber boots,

Only pair left in my size

When I got at last to the village shop

In the first snowflakes yesterday.

Sitting on the park bench quite alone

To read your letter once again, and finally

Deposit it in the rubbish bin, where it can do me no harm.

Life Renewed

Old Man feeds the pigeons every day.
Magpies hunt between the leaves
Beneath the oaks. Sparrows dip
And peck-pick grass seeds.
Gulls turn above. Geese honk
On their V-shaped migration. Down below
Old Man pulls close his yellow oilskin coat
And cap. Who needs more friends?
He asks himself.

Soaking through to her skin,
Miranda pulls her cardigan around her.
Silk grasps her body, clammy, cold and wet.
She has no home, no money, and no hope,
No bed, no box, no socks, no covering.

"Come," Old Man says. She shivers.
Sparrows too say, "Go with him
And trust him," so she does
Passing the fountain, flower-beds,
Swings, the holes where cricket stumps
Were pushed into the ground.

She doesn't ask his name or history.
He doesn't ask the reason she is here.
He's eighty, and he's found a life renewed.

The Missing Muse

Why can I not find inspiration
In the immobility of old age
Now that there is nothing new to see
From closely curtained windows
Even in the passing of seasons
Overlooking fenced short stretches of evergreen?

Even if nothing new stimulates, evergreen
Memories provide pictures which are inspiration
If I can convert my eyes to windows
Back beyond the present age
Regardless of the changing seasons
Between what I now and what I then could see.

But for long periods I find no scenes to see
And fill my time with routines evergreen
Unchanging through the seasons
My major concentration is the inspiration
And exhalation by which I count my age
Ensuring open tubes and veins and windows

By these means I can retain the windows
That are sufficient for me still to see
Through others' words developments of the ages
Retaining ever fewer of the evergreen
Conventions, even meanings, on which past inspiration
Carries lives buoyantly through culture's seasons

Now likes are born on 'phones in shorter seasons
Which trend and die in days, in windows
Lending life to children oozing inspiration
Who speak to millions whom they never see
Only the regularity of their rhythms seem evergreen
Unchanging as their faces and apparent age

Will they, at four-score years of age,
Look back, observe life's seasons
In their contrasts, or perceive only lives evergreen,
Continuous as viewed through teenaged windows?
Some will remember, some will calmly see
The offerings of unique inspiration

> Time passes, and the evergreen of each uncertain age
> Provides a different inspiration as the seasons
> Parade before the windows we may see.

Hoots in Boots

The hooter on my scooter doesn't work.
Once having found the pack of plasters just within my reach,
I need a three-point turn to look for pills
And can do that without the woman close behind
Having a heart attack. I no longer squeak!
But how does she stay calm when, in the street,
A van reverses, squad cars scream along the road beside her,
Burglar alarms above the closing shops
Blare orange light and claxon to confirm
They're working? I feel good.
At least I do not add to all the strife
Of modern, noisy, blaring, screeching life.

The Internet

The Internet is a gangling youth
Outstripped its parents in a flash
Knows more than anyone ever did
When it was born. It makes a dash
If asked a question, cosmic dog
Rounding up answers like a million sheep
All needing to be seen. A slog
Through irrelevance. Also it speaks
Its own language – who understands? –
Only the others who, being geeks,
Can't wait to join in with their dire advice
Always apart from where one might apply
Whatever they might say. Then a surprise –
It works!! Oh, how did that happen? Who knows?
And who could repeat the success? I don't suppose
I can find it again, whether tomorrow or never,
Or perhaps I have lost it, trying to be too clever.

Are You In My Bubble?

Family, neighbour, colleague, friend,
Office, classroom, church hall, blend
Of contacts known from years before.
The need to hug is deep and sore.

No more drop-ins, shopping sprees,
Coffee mornings when we tease
And joke about each others' tastes,
Poke fun at our expanding waists.

Have you sneezed or coughed today?
Children, stop that rough horseplay!
Can you smell the fertiliser?
Can you see behind that visor?

Lock-down loneliness is gross.
All those lovely people close
And yet untouchable for weeks,
Just waves allowed, and distant shrieks.

Tomorrow

Once, tomorrow came, always different from today
Regularly, as the sun turned and the buses ran
To the timetable of one's own responsibilities
And those imposed

Once he went as he chose to do
Walking, cycling, driving, flying, catching trains
Down the street to the corner or
Across continents

There would be a new book tomorrow
A new gap in the world to explore
New food to taste, new cloth to touch
New him to be

He's done all that now. Bones ache, joints scrunch
Now he lurches from chair to table,
Glad when pride admits it's time for bed
But fears for tomorrow

Uncertain

I'm not sure how to hold my face

        when I suck a lemon.

Everyone says a lemon's bitter.

        I've tasted bitter many times before

And held my face neutral

        neither giving out or holding back

whether I know or not how to accept the pain

        or even care how long it's going to last

Lemons, words, gestures, turnings away, ignorings

        all bite, especially where my skin is soft

from earlier strikes that left their marks and hurts.

        Perhaps how I hold my face depends

on how much trust I feel as I pour out

        a pinch of serious poison for you

after all these years of getting by

        doing my duty, arranging, transporting, defending,

deferring, accepting, letting you choose or decline.

Falling

I was always clumsy.
Moving on my feet, my ankles gave
And down I went.

As I aged, my hips collapsed.
Used a stick, tripped over it,
And down I went.

Paramedics learned the way
To my front door just like their own.
"He's down again," they said.

Physiotherapists gave me equipment,
Frames and walkers, things to stand
And things to sit
And things to get to bed,
And still I fell.
"Just try again," they said.

But I gave up, and left my home,
Moved into care with all my gear.
I haven't fallen here just yet.
"You will," my conscience says.

Poor Kettle

My kettle feels abandoned
Almost
    Except when Jim comes round
To organise me and do odd jobs
And make himself a coffee
Filling the kettle for just one cup
And blow the environment

A bit since
    My kettle was always boiling
Eight cups a day and water for the veg
Now I can no longer safely carry
Hot water in a beaker
So for days
    My faithful kettle simply gathers dust instead

To Everything I Own

To everything I own, I love you.
That's why you're here.
Even when I moved and downsized
And dumped so many shared and precious things
In my greatest of all losses,
I could not let you go.
Now we are in two rooms instead of eight.
Now you are crowded together
Like people at a demo.
Now statues jostle, books lie sideways,
Chairs and tables push against each other,
But every one of you were hers, not mine,
And, now I am alone, you bring me love.

Index of Titles

Index of First Lines

FÜR AUTOREN A HEART FOR AUTHORS À L'ÉCOUTE DES AUTEURS MIA KAPΔIA ΓIA ΣYΓΓ
FÖR FÖRFATTARE UN CORAZÓN POR LOS AUTORES YAZARLARIMIZA GÖNÜL VERELIM SZ
PER AUTORI ET HJERTE FOR FORFATTERE EEN HART VOOR SCHRIJVERS TEMOS OS AUTO
ZDINKÉRT SERCE DLA AUTORÓW EIN HERZ FÜR AUTOREN A HEART FOR AUTHORS À L'ÉCOU
ÇÃO ВСЕЙ ДУШОЙ К АВТОРАМ ETT HJÄRTA FÖR FÖRFATTARE Á LA ESCUCHA DE LOS AUTC
KAPΔIA ΓIA ΣYΓΓPAΦEIΣ UN CUORE PER AUTORI ET HJERTE FOR FORFATTERE EEN
ZÔINKÉRT SERCE DLA AUTORÓW EIN HERZ FÜ
CÃO ВСЕЙ ДУШОЙ К АВТОРАМ ETT HJÄRTA FÖ

The author

Robert was a member of the University of Cambridge Spitzbergen expedition, 1965 and undertook research in Libya in 1966–67.

After graduation he lectured in environmental sciences at the Universities of London and Exeter before joining the UK Civil Service. He later spent 7 years as a management consultant, working with central and local government organisations in the UK, Bulgaria and Hungary and with major manufacturing companies in Belgium, Germany, and the USA.

He began writing again after retiring. His earlier poetry collection Late Starter was published in 2018. He has won prizes and commendations in the Solihull Writer's Workshop annual poetry and fiction competitions and has published poems in the quarterly anthologies of the Moseley-based Cannon Poets group. 11 of his short stories are online at www.cafelit.co.uk. His novel A Magic Flight was published in September 2022.

The publisher

> *He who stops getting better stops being good.*

This is the motto of novum publishing, and our focus is on finding new manuscripts, publishing them and offering long-term support to the authors.
Our publishing house was founded in 1997, and since then it has become THE expert for new authors and has won numerous awards.

Our editorial team will peruse each manuscript within a few weeks free of charge and without obligation.

You will find more information about novum publishing and our books on the internet:

www.novum-publishing.co.uk